1/12 OX   3/09

SUPER
SANDCASTLE
Let's Look A to Z

Alcott
to
Zaharias

SAN DIEGO PUBLIC LIBRARY
CHILDREN'S ROOM

Famous Women from A to Z

Mary Elizabeth Salzmann

Consulting Editor, Diane Craig, M.A./Reading Specialist

3 1336 08093 4343

ABDO
Publishing Company

Published by ABDO Publishing Company, 8000 West 78th Street, Edina, Minnesota 55439. Copyright © 2009 by Abdo Consulting Group, Inc. International copyrights reserved in all countries. No part of this book may be reproduced in any form without written permission from the publisher. Super SandCastle™ is a trademark and logo of ABDO Publishing Company.

Printed in the United States.

Editor: Pam Price
Content Developer: Nancy Tuminelly
Cover and Interior Design and Production: Colleen Dolphin, Mighty Media
Photo Credits: The Bancroft Library, University of California, Berkeley; Corbis Images; Getty Images; Michael Ochs Archives/Getty Images; Time & Life Pictures/Getty Images; Roger Viollet/Getty Images; Mount Holyoke College Archives and Special Collections; Smith College Archives, Smith College; Shutterstock

Library of Congress Cataloging-in-Publication Data

Salzmann, Mary Elizabeth, 1968-

 Alcott to Zaharias : famous women from A to Z / Mary Elizabeth Salzmann.

 p. cm. -- (Let's look A to Z)

 ISBN 978-1-60453-010-0

 1. Women--Biography--Juvenile literature. I. Title.

 CT3207.A24 2008

 920.72--dc22

                  2007050948

Super SandCastle™ books are created by a team of professional educators, reading specialists, and content developers around five essential components— phonemic awareness, phonics, vocabulary, text comprehension, and fluency— to assist young readers as they develop reading skills and strategies and increase their general knowledge. All books are written, reviewed, and leveled for guided reading, early reading intervention, and Accelerated Reader® programs for use in shared, guided, and independent reading and writing activities to support a balanced approach to literacy instruction.

About Super SandCastle™

Bigger Books for Emerging Readers Grades K–4

Created for library, classroom, and at-home use, Super SandCastle™ books support and engage young readers as they develop and build literacy skills and will increase their general knowledge about the world around them. Super SandCastle™ books are part of SandCastle™, the leading preK–3 imprint for emerging and beginning readers. Super SandCastle™ features a larger trim size for more reading fun.

Let Us Know

Super SandCastle™ would like to hear your stories about reading this book. What was your favorite page? Was there something hard that you needed help with? Share the ups and downs of learning to read. We want to hear from you! Send us an e-mail.

sandcastle@abdopublishing.com

Contact us for a complete list of SandCastle™, Super SandCastle™, and other nonfiction and fiction titles from ABDO Publishing Company.

www.abdopublishing.com • 8000 West 78th Street Edina, MN 55439 • 800-800-1312 • 952-831-1632 fax

This fun and informative series employs illustrated definitions to introduce emerging readers to an alphabet of words in various topic areas. Each page combines words with corresponding images and descriptive sentences to encourage learning and knowledge retention. AlphagalorZ inspires young readers to find out more about the subjects that most interest them!

The "Guess what?" feature expands the reading and learning experience by offering additional information and fascinating facts about specific words or concepts. The "More Words" section provides additional related A to Z vocabulary words that develop and increase reading comprehension.

These books are appropriate for library, classroom, and home use.

Aa

Louisa May Alcott

1832-1888

Louisa May Alcott was an author who published many poems, stories, and books.

Her most popular book is *Little Women.*

Guess what?

Little Women was first published in 1868.

Lucille Ball

1911-1989

Lucille Ball was an American movie and television actress.

She is best known for her starring role in the TV show *I Love Lucy.*

"The more things you do, the more you can do."

Bb

5

Marie Curie

Marie Curie received
two Nobel Prizes,
one in physics and
one in chemistry.

She did experiments
with radioactive materials.

1867-1934

Cc

Guess what?

Marie Curie was the
first person to receive
two Nobel Prizes!

Emily Dickinson

"A word is dead
When it is said,
Some say.
I say it just
Begins to live
That day."

1830–1886

Emily Dickinson wrote more than 1,700 poems, but only a few of them were published while she was alive.

Today she is considered one of the greatest American poets.

Amelia Earhart

Amelia Earhart was the first woman to fly an airplane alone across the Atlantic Ocean.

She was also the first woman to fly nonstop across the United States.

Ee

1897-1937

"The most effective way to do it, is to do it."

Anne Frank

Guess what?

Anne Frank's diary has been published in more than 60 languages.

Anne Frank and her family hid from the Nazis in secret rooms for two years.

She wrote a diary about her life during her time in hiding.

Ff

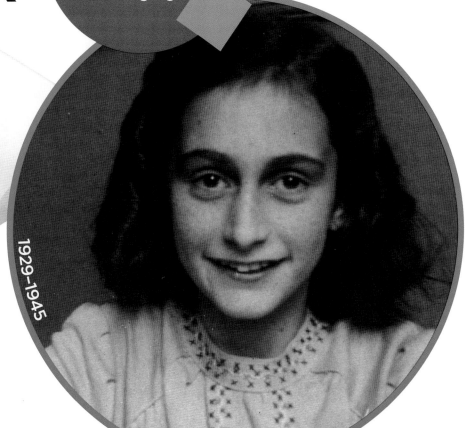

1929-1945

9

Indira Gandhi

"You cannot shake hands with a clenched fist."

Gg

1917-1984

When she was a teenager, Indira Gandhi led a children's movement to help end English rule of India.

In 1966, she became the third prime minister of India.

1915-1959

Hh

Billie Holiday

Billie Holiday was a jazz singer.

She got her start singing in clubs in Harlem, New York City.

Guess what?

Billie Holiday was nicknamed Lady Day.

1944–2007

Molly Ivins

Molly Ivins was a journalist, columnist, and author.

She was known for using humor to write about politics.

Guess what?

Molly Ivins wrote more than 10 books, and her column appeared in 400 newspapers.

li

Janis Joplin

Janis Joplin was an influential blues and rock singer.

One of her biggest hits is the song "Me and Bobby McGee."

1943–1970

"Don't compromise yourself. You're all you've got."

JJ

Kk

Helen Keller

Although Helen Keller couldn't see or hear, she learned to read and write.

She went to college, wrote books, and helped the disabled.

1880-1968

"We can do anything we want to if we stick to it long enough."

Juliette Gordon Low lost most of her hearing ability when she was in her twenties.

1860–1927

Juliette Gordon Low

In 1912, Juliette Gordon Low started the Girl Scouts.

There were 18 girls at her first Girl Scout meeting in Savannah, Georgia.

Guess what.?

Maria Montessori was the first female doctor in Italy.

1870–1952

Mm

Maria Montessori

Maria Montessori was the Italian doctor and educator who started the Montessori schools.

She studied the way children grow and learn.

She used what she learned to develop better ways to teach children.

Florence Nightingale

"I attribute my success to this— I never gave or took any excuse."

Florence Nightingale was an English nurse who cared for wounded soldiers.

She started the Nightingale Training School for nurses in 1860.

1820–1910

Guess what?

Annie Oakley donated most of the money she earned to charities that helped women and children.

1860–1926

Annie Oakley

Annie Oakley was an excellent sharpshooter.

She performed in Buffalo Bill's Wild West show from 1885 to 1901.

Pp

1913–2005

Rosa Parks

In 1955, Rosa Parks was arrested when she refused to give her seat on a bus to a white man.

She stood up for her rights and worked to get segregation laws changed.

"Each person must live their life as a model for others."

Qq

Harriet Quimby

1875-1912

Harriet Quimby was the first female licensed pilot in the United States.

In 1912, she became the first woman pilot to fly solo across the English Channel.

Guess what?

Harriet Quimby designed a purple outfit with a hood that she wore whenever she flew.

Wilma Rudolph

"The most important aspect is to be yourself and have confidence in yourself."

1940–1994

Wilma Rudolph had polio and wore braces on her legs as a child. However, she got better and became a track star.

She won three gold medals in the 1960 Olympic Games.

Sacagawea

Sacagawea was a Native American woman who helped guide the Lewis and Clark trip from North Dakota to the Pacific Ocean.

She helped them trade and communicate with the Native Americans they met along the way.

Ss

Guess what ?

Sacagawea is on some U.S. dollar coins.

about 1786-1812

about 1820–1913

Harriet Tubman

Harriet Tubman was born a slave in Maryland but escaped to Philadelphia in 1849.

She worked for the Underground Railroad, helping many other slaves gain their freedom.

"I never ran my train off the track, and I never lost a passenger."

Tt

Uu

Yoshiko Uchida

1921-1992

Yoshiko Uchida wrote books for children and teenagers.

Her stories are about growing up Japanese-American.

Guess what..?

Yoshiko Uchida started writing stories when she was 10 years old.

Guess what?

Queen Victoria kept a diary throughout her life.

1819-1901

Queen Victoria

Queen Victoria became Queen of England when she was 18 years old.

She ruled for 63 years, and the time of her reign is called the Victorian era.

Vv

Laura Ingalls Wilder

Laura Ingalls Wilder wrote 11 books about her life on the American frontier.

Two of her books are *Little House in the Big Woods* and *Little House on the Prairie*.

"It is the sweet, simple things of life which are the real ones after all."

1867-1957

Ww

1921–2000

Xx

Xide Xie

Xide Xie was a Chinese scientist and professor.

She did experiments with different kinds of metals.

Guess what?

Xide Xie was president of Fudan University in China.

Anne Sewell Young

Anne Sewell Young was one of the first woman astronomers.

She taught at Mount Holyoke College in Massachusetts.

Guess what?

Anne Young also wrote articles about astronomy for the local newspaper.

Yy

1871–1961

Mildred "Babe" Didrikson Zaharias

Babe Zaharias was named Female Athlete of the Year six times by the Associated Press.

At the 1932 Olympic Games, she won two gold medals and one silver medal in track and field.

Later she started playing golf and won more than 80 tournaments.

1911-1956

"You can't win them all—but you can try."

Glossary

astronomer – someone who studies objects and matter outside the earth's atmosphere, such as planets, moons, and stars.

astronomy – the study of objects and matter outside the earth's atmosphere, such as planets, moons, and stars.

athlete – someone who is good at sports or games that require strength, speed, or agility.

columnist – someone who writes an article that appears regularly in a newspaper or a magazine.

communicate – to share ideas, information, or feelings.

design – to plan how something will appear or work.

develop – to grow or change over time.

donate – to give a gift in order to help others.

educator – a teacher.

experiment – a scientific test done to discover information.

female – being of the sex that can produce eggs or give birth. Mothers are female.

frontier – the land at or beyond the edge of a developed area.

influential – having the ability to cause change without using force.

journalist – a person who describes events and reports facts.

licensed – having received legal or official permission to do a particular thing.

material – the substance something is made of, such as metal, fabric, or plastic.

outfit – a set of clothes worn for a special occasion or purpose.

physics – the science of how energy and objects affect each other.

pilot – a person who operates an aircraft or a ship.

popular – liked by many people.

radioactive – able to give off rays of energy or particles by breaking atoms apart.

role – a part played by an actor.

segregation – the separation of an individual or a group from a larger group.

sharpshooter – someone who can shoot a gun accurately over and over.

tournament – a series of contests or games played to win a championship.

More Famous Women!

Can you learn about these women too?

Aaliyah	Katharine Hepburn	Joan Lowery Nixon
Jane Addams	Grace Murray Hopper	Mary Teresa Norton
Marian Anderson	Zora Neale Hurston	Georgia O'Keeffe
Susan B. Anthony	Jill Ireland	Pocahontas
Josephine Baker	Frances Wisebart Jacobs	Beatrix Potter
Clara Barton	Mary Harris "Mother" Jones	Eleanor Roosevelt
Frances Hodgson Burnett	Barbara Jordan	Betsy Ross
Mary Ann Shadd Cary	Grace Kelly	Josephine St. Pierre Ruffin
Mary Cassatt	Maggie Kuhn	Bessie Smith
Bessie Coleman	Susette La Flesche	Harriet Beecher Stowe
Paula Danziger	Dorothea Lange	Anne Sullivan
Dorothy Day	Astrid Lindgren	Mother Teresa
Trudy Ederle	Patricia A. Locke	Sojourner Truth
Ella Fitzgerald	Margaret Mead	Maribel Vinson
Betty Friedan	Golda Meir	Annie Dodge Wauneka
Althea Gibson	Patsy Takemoto Mink	Sarah Winnemucca
Katharine Graham	Anna Mary "Grandma" Moses	Chien-Shiung Wu